PRAYERSCRIPTS
Speaking God's Word Back to You

THE PRAYER OF JABEZ

NO MORE PAIN

30 Days of Prayers For

BREAKING FREE FROM SUFFERING
INTO WHOLENESS

CYRIL OPOKU

No More Pain: Breaking Free from Suffering into Wholeness

© 2025 Cyril Opoku. *PrayerScripts*. All rights reserved.

Published by *Quest Publications*

ISBN: 978-1-988439-85-3

Cover design by *Quest Publications (questpublications@outlook.com)*

Unless otherwise indicated, all Scripture quotations are taken from the World English Bible WEB, which is in the public domain. For more information, visit: www.worldenglish.bible

This book is a work of devotional encouragement. It is not intended to replace biblical study, pastoral counsel, or professional therapy.

Printed in the United States of America.

First Edition: August 2025

For more books like this, visit *PrayerScripts:* https://prayerscripts.org

CONTENTS

Preface v

How to Use This Book vii

Introduction x

Week 1: Naming the Wound 1

   Day 1:   Enlarge My Territory 2

   Day 2:   Restore My Joy.. 4

   Day 3:   Wounded Yet Healed 6

   Day 4:   Near To The Broken 8

   Day 5:   Weeping Turned Into Dancing 9

   Day 6:   Comfort My People.. 11

   Day 7:   Great Is Your Faithfulness 13

Week 2: Nearness & Comfort... 14

   Day 8:   The Father of Mercies 15

   Day 9:   As A Mother Comforts................................... 17

   Day 10:   Joy in the Wasteland 19

   Day 11:   Engraved in His Hands................................... 21

   Day 12:   Binding the Brokenhearted 23

   Day 13:   Boldly Before the Throne 24

   Day 14:   When You Pass Through 26

Week 3: Healing & Restoration.. 28

   Day 15:   Beauty for Ashes.. 29

   Day 16:   Restored to Health 31

   Day 17:   The Lord Who Heals You 33

   Day 18:   Crowned with Loving Kindness...................... 35

   Day 19:   Years Restored 37

   Day 20:   Prayer of Faith 39

   Day 21:   By His Stripes 41

   Day 22:   The God Who Hears...................................... 43

Week 4: Wholeness & Hope 45

Day 23:   Everlasting Light of Joy.. 46

Day 24:   Joy Instead of Weeping 48

Day 25:   Overflow of Gladness... 50

Day 26:   Rest for the Weary.. 52

Day 27:   No More Tears Forever 54

Day 28:   All Things Work Together 56

Day 29:   Restorer of My Soul.. 58

Day 30:   He Took My Infirmities 59

Epilogue *61*

Encourage Others with Your Story... *63*

More from PrayerScripts.. *64*

PREFACE

"Oh that you would bless me indeed, and enlarge my
territory, that your hand would be with me, and that you
would keep me from evil, that I may not cause pain!"
— 1 Chronicles 4:10 WEB

From the first day I encountered the story of Jabez, his prayer
became a mirror for my own heart—a prayer that dared to
reach beyond limits, that sought God's hand in every corner
of life. Over the years, I have walked through seasons of quiet
struggle and times when pain seemed to linger like an unwelcome
companion. This book is born out of that journey, a journey from
wounds to wellness, from sorrow to peace. Each page has been
prayer-tested in my own life, shaped by Scripture, and inspired by
the unshakable promise that God desires to heal, restore, and break
the cycles of suffering.

As you step into this book, you are stepping into a prophetic
invitation to let God's presence saturate every aching place in your
life and family. Here, prayer becomes a bridge from fear to faith,
from isolation to divine companionship. It is my hope that as you
pray these prayers, you will feel the tangible nearness of God, the
kind of nearness that binds up broken hearts, dismantles
strongholds of pain, and establishes you firmly in His peace.

This is a space to wrestle, to declare, and to receive. It is a space
where pain meets God's power, where grief becomes a testimony,
and where the hope of wholeness becomes reality. I encourage you
to take your time, speak these prayers aloud, meditate on the

Scriptures, and allow the Holy Spirit to breathe life into your weary places. Healing is not a one-time event—it is a journey, and God walks it with you every step of the way.

Under His Healing Hand,
Cyril O. *(Illinois, August 2025)*

HOW TO USE THIS BOOK

This book is designed as a daily companion to guide you into a prophetic lifestyle of prayer. This is a prayer journey meant to position you to walk in the fullness of God's promises. Here's how to make the most of it:

1. Dedicate a Daily Time:

Set aside a consistent time each day to engage with the prayer for that day. Treat this as sacred time with God, where distractions are minimized, and your heart is fully focused on communion with Him. Ten to twenty minutes daily is sufficient to meditate on the Scripture, pray, and receive revelation.

2. Begin with Scripture Reflection:

Each day begins with a carefully selected Scripture. Read it slowly, meditate on its meaning, and let the Holy Spirit illuminate how it applies to your life. Allow the Word to penetrate your spirit and prepare you to pray from a place of faith and expectancy.

3. Pray the Guided Prayer:

Use the prayer provided as a framework, allowing it to resonate with your own words and personal circumstances. Speak each declaration with authority and confidence, fully believing that God is enlarging your borders, breaking limitations, and establishing your territory. You may also pause to personalize the prayer for your specific family, career, or ministry needs.

- **Make It Personal**

  These prayers are written in the first person so you can make them your own. Speak them aloud, inserting the names of your family members, your workplace, your church, or your city where applicable. The more you personalize the prayer, the more you will sense its power shaping your reality.

- **Pray with Authority**

  These are not timid requests; they are bold decrees. Lift your voice as a covenant child of God, covered by the blood of Jesus and backed by heaven's authority. When you pray, do so with confidence that Christ has already won the victory on your behalf.

- **Leave Room for the Holy Spirit**

  These written prayers are a guide, not a limit. As you pray, pause to listen. The Holy Spirit may give you prophetic words, insights, or specific instructions. Follow His lead. Allow Him to expand the prayer, add declarations, or guide you into deeper intercession.

4. Journal Your Insights:

Keep a notebook or journal to record any thoughts, revelations, or confirmations you receive during prayer. Writing down what God speaks to you helps solidify understanding and creates a record of breakthrough and growth over time.

5. Repeat as Needed:

Some prayers or themes may need to be revisited multiple times. Answer to prayer is progressive; the more you engage with these prayers in faith, the greater the manifestation in your life and household. You can return to this book at any season to reinforce your victory and dominion.

6. Live in Expectancy:

Prayer is only one part of walking in enlargement—your actions, faith, and obedience amplify the power of these prayers. Move boldly into opportunities, embrace the doors God opens, and live with a confident expectation that God is answering your prayer beyond what you can see or imagine.

By following this guide daily, you will cultivate a lifestyle of prayer and kingdom impact. Let this book be your companion as you step into the new dimensions God has destined for you.

INTRODUCTION

"Jabez called on the God of Israel, saying, 'Oh that you would bless me indeed, and enlarge my border! Let your hand be with me, and keep me from evil, that I may not cause pain!' God granted him that which he requested."
—1 Chronicles 4:10 WEB

Pain is a language every human understands. It arrives uninvited, sometimes through sudden loss or betrayal, other times through prolonged hardship that wears the soul down. It creeps into the mind, lingers in the body, and settles into the heart. Pain not only wounds—it whispers. It tells us that sorrow is permanent, that healing is impossible, that joy is a memory we will never reclaim.

But the truth of God's Word interrupts those lies: **pain is not the end of the story**. The Lord promises healing for the brokenhearted, comfort for those who mourn, and restoration for every place the enemy has stolen from us. He has sworn to turn mourning into dancing, ashes into beauty, and sorrow into songs of joy. Pain may be part of your journey, but it is not your destination.

The prayer of Jabez in 1 Chronicles 4:10 anchors this truth. Though his very name meant sorrow, Jabez cried out to God and asked for deliverance from pain. God answered him. That same God is still answering today. No matter what has marked your past or tried to define your present, your future can be rewritten by the power of His presence.

This book is a journey—a prophetic walk from wounds into wellness, from brokenness into restoration, from pain into peace. Each week focuses on a vital part of this transformation:

- **Week 1: Naming the Wound** – Acknowledging pain with honesty and surrender. Healing begins where denial ends.
- **Week 2: Nearness & Comfort** – Encountering God's presence in suffering, where His Spirit becomes strength and His voice brings calm.
- **Week 3: Healing & Restoration** – Trusting the Lord to repair what was shattered and to breathe life into what seemed lost forever.
- **Week 4: Wholeness & Hope** – Stepping into lasting freedom, joy, and renewed expectation for the future.

Every Scripture, every prayer, every prophetic word in these pages is designed to confront the cycle of sorrow and release the healing power of God. The cross of Christ ensures that suffering does not have the final word. He bore our griefs, carried our sorrows, and broke the power of pain through His sacrifice.

As you walk through these chapters, do not hold back. Pour out your heart. Let God touch the places you've hidden, the wounds you've carried, and the memories that still ache. This is where the exchange takes place. Grief gives way to joy. Fear gives way to peace. Wounds give way to wholeness.

No more pain is God's promise of restoration. It is a declaration that sorrow's time is up and a new season has begun. The night has ended. The dawn is here. Step forward—your journey into healing starts now.

WEEK 1:
NAMING THE WOUND

Theme: Honest Lament & Surrender.

Healing begins with truth. Too often, we bury our pain under layers of denial, distraction, or forced strength. We pretend we are fine, even as wounds continue to bleed in silence. But God cannot heal what we refuse to reveal. The first step toward wholeness is naming the wound—acknowledging where it hurts, how it has shaped us, and surrendering it honestly before the Lord.

Scripture is full of laments. Job cried out in anguish. David poured out his tears in the Psalms. Even Jesus wept openly at Lazarus' tomb. Honest lament is not weakness; it is worship. It is the act of bringing our raw and unfiltered pain to the only One who can bear it. God does not despise your tears—He bottles them. He does not reject your sorrow—He welcomes it as the place where His comfort can begin to flow.

This week is about removing the mask. It is about surrendering denial, shame, and silence. It is about calling pain by its name and bringing it to the God who heals. As you pray through these Scriptures, expect chains to break simply by the power of truth. Naming the wound is not staying stuck in it—it is the doorway into freedom.

DAY 1

ENLARGE MY TERRITORY

"Jabez called on the God of Israel, saying, 'Oh that you
would bless me indeed, and enlarge my border! Let your
hand be with me, and keep me from evil, that I may not
cause pain!' God granted him that which he requested."
— 1 Chronicles 4:10 WEB

O God of Israel, I cry to You as Jabez did. You are the God who
transforms pain into purpose and sorrow into strength. Today, I
declare that no chain of affliction will define me or my household.
Every cycle of grief, disappointment, and inherited sorrow is
broken by the power of Your hand. I refuse to be bound to
yesterday's wounds, for You are enlarging my territory and making
me fruitful in the land of my affliction.

Father, stretch out Your hand upon my life and upon my family.
Where there has been pain, let there now be prosperity. Where
there have been tears, let there now be testimonies. Drive out every
spirit of shame and rejection that has whispered against our destiny.
Every curse assigned to keep us small and hidden is shattered in the
mighty name of Jesus.

Lord, as You increase my border, I surrender my wounds to You. I
release bitterness, unforgiveness, and sorrow at Your feet. I choose
to walk in the wholeness of Your blessing. Let the oil of Your favor
rest upon me, and let every enemy of my soul be silenced under the
weight of Your glory.

I decree that from this day forward, my life will not be marked by pain but by peace, not by sorrow but by songs of deliverance. I step boldly into the enlargement of territory You have ordained for me and my family.

In Jesus' name, Amen.

DAY 2

RESTORE MY JOY

"Let me hear joy and gladness, that the bones which you have broken may rejoice. Restore to me the joy of your salvation. Uphold me with a willing spirit."
— Psalms 51:8, 12 WEB

Merciful Father, I come before You as David came, laying bare my brokenness. You are the One who knows every crack in my soul and every wound in my spirit. Today I confess that I cannot mend myself, but I yield to Your hand that brings restoration. Breathe upon my dry places until joy rises again like morning light after a storm.

Lord, silence the voice of the accuser that seeks to drown me in guilt and shame. Every dark memory and every lingering regret must bow to the blood of Jesus. I decree that my family and I will not be chained to the sins of the past, but we will be upheld by the righteousness of Christ. We will rejoice in salvation that no enemy can steal.

Father, restore laughter where mourning has lived. Let the bones that felt crushed under sorrow now leap with rejoicing. Wash over my mind with the river of gladness. Heal every scar that the enemy used to keep me in cycles of pain. The joy of the Lord is rising as my strength, breaking the heaviness that tried to weigh me down.

I yield to Your Spirit to uphold me. Make me willing to walk forward, willing to embrace freedom, willing to choose life. Lord, restore not only my joy but also the joy of my family. Let our household be known as a place of gladness, a house filled with Your presence.

In Jesus' name, Amen.

DAY 3

WOUNDED YET HEALED

"Behold, happy is the man whom God corrects. Therefore do not despise the chastening of the Almighty. For he wounds and binds up. He injures and his hands make whole."
— Job 5:17-18 WEB

Almighty Healer, I bow before Your throne in surrender. I acknowledge that even in Your correction there is love, and even in Your wounding there is healing. What the enemy meant for destruction, You are using as a tool for my restoration. I embrace Your refining fire and trust Your hand that binds up every wound.

Father, I decree that every demonic assignment of prolonged pain is overturned. The enemy will not keep my family in endless cycles of affliction. Though we may have been bruised by life's trials, Your hands are making us whole. You are binding up our hearts with cords of compassion, knitting together what was torn apart.

Lord, I release bitterness toward the process of correction. I surrender the resentment that tried to poison my spirit. Instead, I accept the healing that flows from Your hands. You are removing every splinter of grief, every shard of rejection, and every sting of loss. Your touch is transforming our brokenness into testimonies of wholeness.

I declare today that our wounds will not define us; Your healing will. My household will testify that the Lord who wounds also makes alive, the One who breaks also rebuilds. No weapon formed against us shall prevail, for we are wrapped in the covering of Your mercy. In Jesus' name, Amen.

DAY 4

NEAR TO THE BROKEN

"Yahweh is near to those who have a broken heart, and
saves those who have a crushed spirit."
— Psalm 34:18 WEB

Faithful God, I lift my voice to declare Your nearness. You have
never abandoned me, even when my heart was shattered and my
spirit crushed. In the midst of sorrow, Your presence has been my
hiding place. Today, I decree that no power of darkness can separate
me or my family from the saving embrace of Your love.

Lord, I acknowledge my brokenness before You. I do not hide my
pain, for You are not ashamed of my weakness. Instead, You draw
near with compassion. I surrender every hidden wound, every
silent tear, every unspoken ache. By the authority of Your Word, I
reject the spirit of despair that tried to choke the breath of hope
from me.

Father, surround my family with Your saving presence. Rescue us
from the grip of generational sorrow and the traps of depression.
Where the enemy has crushed spirits with hopelessness, breathe
new life. Where hearts have been wounded by betrayal or loss,
mend them with Your eternal kindness.

I decree that we will rise from brokenness into strength. Though the
enemy desired our downfall, You have turned our mourning into
dancing. The shadow of grief is lifting, and the light of Your
salvation is breaking forth in our home. In Jesus' name, Amen.

DAY 5

WEEPING TURNED INTO DANCING

"For his anger is but for a moment. His favor is for a lifetime. Weeping may stay for the night, but joy comes in the morning… You have turned my mourning into dancing for me. You have removed my sackcloth, and clothed me with gladness."
— Psalms 30:5, 11 WEB

Mighty Deliverer, I proclaim today that the night of weeping has ended, and the dawn of joy has come. Though sorrow sought to linger in my house, Your favor has arisen with power. I decree that the garments of mourning are stripped away, and a new robe of gladness is wrapped around me and my family.

Lord, I renounce every spirit of heaviness that tried to make a permanent dwelling in our lives. The season of pain is over, the chains of sorrow are broken, and the grip of despair is loosed. The sound of lament is silenced, and the dance of victory is released in my household.

Father, turn every bitter tear into a testimony of triumph. Where the enemy has mocked us with loss, clothe us with gladness that cannot be stolen. Replace every night of anguish with mornings filled with songs of deliverance. Let joy overflow until it drowns out every whisper of sorrow.

I declare that my family will not remain in sackcloth. We are rising as a people clothed with light, clothed with laughter, clothed with everlasting favor. The voice of praise will echo in our dwelling, testifying that the Lord has turned our mourning into dancing.

In Jesus' name, Amen.

DAY 6

COMFORT MY PEOPLE

"Comfort, comfort my people," says your God. "Speak comfortably to Jerusalem; and call out to her, that her warfare is accomplished, that her iniquity is pardoned, that she has received of Yahweh's hand double for all her sins."
— Isaiah 40:1-2 WEB

God of All Comfort, I lift my heart in gratitude that You have spoken peace to me. My warfare is accomplished, and my iniquity pardoned by the blood of Jesus. I declare that the season of endless battles is finished, and the dawn of restoration has arrived. You are comforting me and my family with Your unfailing love.

Lord, I renounce every spirit of warfare that has tried to prolong its stay. I silence every voice that declares perpetual struggle. I decree that the battle is over, and the banner of peace is lifted over my home. Where there has been pain, let there be pardon. Where there has been warfare, let there be double restoration.

Father, let Your voice of comfort echo louder than the voice of the accuser. Speak tenderly into my wounds, declaring that I am forgiven, healed, and restored. I surrender every scar to Your healing hand, for You are rewriting my story with hope and victory.

I declare that my family will walk in the abundance of Your comfort. The sound of war will no longer define us; the sound of rejoicing will fill our dwelling. The weight of sin and sorrow is lifted, replaced with the double portion of Your blessing.

In Jesus' name, Amen.

DAY 7

GREAT IS YOUR FAITHFULNESS

"It is because of Yahweh's loving kindnesses that we are not consumed, because his compassion doesn't fail. They are new every morning. Great is your faithfulness."
— Lamentations 3:22-23 WEB

Faithful Father, I lift my voice to exalt You, for Your mercies have preserved my life. Though pain threatened to consume me, Your compassion stood as a shield. Today, I declare that every attempt of the enemy to overwhelm my family has failed because of Your unfailing love.

Lord, I rest in the assurance that Your mercies are new every morning. Yesterday's sorrow cannot define today's joy. The cycles of grief are broken by the sunrise of Your faithfulness. I decree that my household is anchored in Your love, unshaken by storms, and untouched by destruction.

Father, I renounce every lie of the enemy that says we will not recover. Your compassion never fails, and Your faithfulness cannot be broken. Where pain tried to linger, mercy has risen. Where sorrow tried to choke hope, new compassion has breathed life.

I declare that every day will testify of Your kindness. My family will awaken not with fear, but with the assurance that mercy has met us again. Great is Your faithfulness to heal, to restore, and to bring us into wholeness. In Jesus' name, Amen.

Week 2:
Nearness & Comfort

Theme: *God's Presence in Our Pain.*

Pain often whispers the lie that God has abandoned us. When sorrow feels overwhelming and prayers seem unanswered, it is easy to believe we are walking alone. Yet the testimony of Scripture is clear: the Lord is near to the brokenhearted, and He saves those crushed in spirit. His presence is not absent in pain—it is most present in the valley.

The God we serve is not distant or indifferent. He comes close. He is the Comforter who sits with us in grief, the Shepherd who walks with us through the valley of the shadow, the Father who gathers His children in His arms. His presence is not just sympathy—it is strength. It is the power that steadies us when everything else shakes.

This week's prayers draw you deeper into the nearness of God. They are an invitation to feel His presence in the very places that hurt. You will discover that comfort is not the absence of pain but the assurance of His companionship in the midst of it. As you lean in, you will find that His presence silences fear, restores hope, and wraps your wounds in the warmth of His peace.

DAY 8

THE FATHER OF MERCIES

"Blessed be the God and Father of our Lord Jesus Christ, the Father of mercies and God of all comfort, who comforts us in all our affliction, that we may be able to comfort those who are in any affliction, through the comfort with which we ourselves are comforted by God."
— 2 Corinthians 1:3-4 WEB

O God of all comfort, I lift my voice with boldness and proclaim that Your mercy has located me and my household today. You are the Father of mercies, the One who bends low to hear the cries of Your children, and the Mighty Deliverer who lifts the burdens of affliction from our shoulders. I decree that no sorrow, no grief, and no pain shall have dominion over me, because You have surrounded me with the power of Your unfailing comfort.

Lord, let the spirit of heaviness be shattered in my life and in my family line. I declare that generational cycles of pain, anguish, and torment are broken by Your hand. Comfort flows into the hidden places of my soul where wounds have lingered. Like oil poured over dry bones, Your presence brings soothing, healing, and restoration until mourning turns into gladness.

I stand in the authority of Christ Jesus and command every demonic oppressor that feeds on grief and loss to flee. By the blood of Jesus, I sever every tie that keeps my family bound to sorrow, and I release divine consolation that strengthens, uplifts, and renews.

Father, let Your mercy be the wall of fire around us, shielding us from the spirit of despair.

I embrace the truth that in the same measure I have been comforted, I shall rise as a vessel of comfort to others. What the enemy meant for pain, You transform into a testimony of deliverance. O Father of mercies, continue to breathe Your peace upon me until wholeness is fully manifest.

In Jesus' name, Amen.

DAY 9

AS A MOTHER COMFORTS

"As one whom his mother comforts, so I will comfort you. You will be comforted in Jerusalem. You will see it, and your heart shall rejoice, and your bones will flourish like the tender grass; and Yahweh's hand will be known among his servants; and he will have indignation against his enemies."
— Isaiah 66:13-14 WEB

Everlasting Father, I exalt You as the Nurturer of my soul. With the gentleness of a mother, You stoop down to embrace me in my pain. I decree this day that I am not forsaken, nor am I abandoned to grief, for Your comforting hand rests upon me and my family. Your nearness is my strength, and Your consolation is the shield that covers every fragile place in my heart.

Lord, let the sound of rejoicing break forth from within me. Cause my heart to leap with joy where despair once lingered. I speak divine flourishing into the bones of my household—every dry place receives life, every weary spirit receives renewal, and every broken dream is resurrected by Your tender mercy.

By the authority of Your Word, I declare that Your indignation rises against every enemy of my soul. The adversary that sought to bind me with sorrow is scattered before Your holy presence. My enemies fall, but I stand upright in Your comfort, rejoicing in the certainty that You have claimed victory for me.

Father, let my life become the testimony of Jerusalem restored—a people clothed with gladness, strengthened in Your presence, and shining with the radiance of Your peace. Your hand is upon me, and no power of darkness shall overturn what You have decreed. I dwell in Your embrace where fear cannot enter, and I rise clothed in joy.

In Jesus' name, Amen.

DAY 10

JOY IN THE WASTELAND

"For Yahweh has comforted Zion. He has comforted all her waste places and has made her wilderness like Eden, and her desert like the garden of Yahweh. Joy and gladness will be found in them, thanksgiving, and the voice of melody... The ransomed of Yahweh will return, and come with singing to Zion; and everlasting joy shall be on their heads. They shall obtain gladness and joy. Sorrow and sighing shall flee away. I, even I, am he who comforts you. Who are you, that you are afraid of man who shall die, and of the son of man who will be made as grass?"
— Isaiah 51:3, 11-13 WEB

Mighty Comforter, I decree that my wastelands are turning into gardens by Your Word. Where sorrow and pain once dominated, You are planting joy, thanksgiving, and songs of deliverance. The wilderness seasons in my life and my family are being transformed into Eden, flourishing with peace and abundance.

Lord, I uproot fear from the soil of my heart. I refuse to tremble before man or yield to the threats of the adversary, for You, the Eternal One, comfort me. I rise with holy boldness to declare that sorrow and sighing have no more authority in my life. By the blood of the Lamb, grief flees, and everlasting joy rests upon my head.

I command every demonic oppressor that seeks to prolong pain in my lineage to be destroyed. No voice of despair shall overshadow the melody of thanksgiving that You are releasing in my household.

Where my family has mourned, we shall now dance. Where we have been silent in grief, our mouths shall overflow with songs of Zion.

Father, I embrace the identity of the ransomed of the Lord. I walk in freedom, clothed with joy that cannot be stolen, sustained by peace that cannot be broken. Your comfort shields me and assures me that pain will not define my destiny. I decree wholeness, restoration, and holy flourishing for me and my bloodline.

In Jesus' name, Amen.

DAY 11

Engraved in His Hands

"Sing, heavens, and be joyful, earth! Break out into singing, mountains, for Yahweh has comforted his people, and will have compassion on his afflicted. But Zion said, 'Yahweh has forsaken me, and the Lord has forgotten me.' Can a woman forget her nursing child, that she should not have compassion on the son of her womb? Yes, these may forget, yet I will not forget you! Behold, I have engraved you on the palms of my hands."
— Isaiah 49:13-16 WEB

Lord, Redeemer of Israel, I declare with confidence that I am not forgotten. Though affliction has tried to convince me that I am forsaken, I decree today that Your compassion defines me. You have engraved me on the palms of Your hands, and my name is etched in the place of covenant love.

Father, I command every lying spirit that whispers abandonment into my heart to be silenced. My destiny is not one of rejection, but of acceptance in the Beloved. No wound of neglect shall dominate my family, for You have comforted us and remembered us with everlasting compassion.

I lift a prophetic song of joy into the atmosphere of my home. Let the heavens sing and the mountains resound, for You are making our lives a testimony of restoration. O God, I decree that the chains of affliction are broken, and my family rises in wholeness, healed by Your unfailing nearness.

Every enemy that sought to isolate me in grief is defeated. No power of hell can erase the engraving of my life upon Your hands. You hold me securely, and Your compassion is stronger than the fiercest sorrow. I rise into joy and wholeness, carried in Your remembrance. In Jesus' name, Amen.

DAY 12

BINDING THE BROKENHEARTED

"He heals the broken in heart, and binds up their wounds."
— Psalm 147:3 WEB

Great Healer, I come before You with a declaration of victory: every broken place in my life and in my family is being healed by Your hand. You are binding up wounds that have lingered through generations, and You are mending hearts that were shattered by loss, betrayal, and pain.

Lord, I command every tormenting spirit that exploits brokenness to depart from my life. No longer shall grief, bitterness, or anguish feed upon the wounds of my soul. I decree supernatural restoration and healing virtue flowing like a river into the deepest parts of my being.

I prophesy that every scar in my family line becomes a testimony of Your redemptive power. Where the enemy sought to divide and destroy, Your hand of compassion is uniting, mending, and strengthening. You are binding up the wounds of rejection, failure, and despair, and replacing them with love, hope, and peace.

Father, I declare that no more pain shall define me, for You have written wholeness into my destiny. Your healing touch secures me, and Your presence comforts me until gladness overtakes sorrow. I am rising, whole and strong, clothed in the fullness of peace You alone provide. In Jesus' name, Amen.

DAY 13

BOLDLY BEFORE THE THRONE

"For we don't have a high priest who can't be touched with the feeling of our infirmities, but one who has been in all points tempted like we are, yet without sin. Let's therefore draw near with boldness to the throne of grace, that we may receive mercy, and may find grace for help in time of need."
— Hebrews 4:15-16 WEB

Lord Jesus, my Great High Priest, I exalt You as the One who understands my pain. You are touched by the feelings of my infirmities, and You stand as my Advocate before the Father. Today I decree that I draw near with boldness, confident that mercy is poured out upon me and my household.

I silence every spirit of condemnation that seeks to distance me from Your throne. By the blood of Jesus, I have access to the holy place where mercy flows like a river and grace strengthens me in weakness. I receive help in my time of need, and I decree that the same mercy becomes a covering for my family.

Lord, I declare that sorrow has no power to isolate me from Your presence. Instead, pain becomes the very place where Your grace is most evident. You have turned what the enemy intended for despair into a pathway of greater intimacy with You.

I rise in authority to command every spiritual adversary to bow to the victory of Christ. No power of darkness can withstand the flow of mercy and grace that covers my life. My family walks in supernatural strength, secured by the intercession of our Great High Priest.

Father, let my life testify that Your throne is not one of judgment for me, but of compassion, nearness, and unfailing help. I rest in Your comfort and rejoice in Your grace.

In Jesus' name, Amen.

DAY 14

WHEN YOU PASS THROUGH

"But now Yahweh who created you, Jacob, and he who formed you, Israel, says: 'Don't be afraid, for I have redeemed you. I have called you by your name. You are mine. When you pass through the waters, I will be with you; and through the rivers, they will not overflow you. When you walk through the fire, you will not be burned, and flame will not scorch you.'"
— Isaiah 43:1-2 WEB

Redeeming God, I lift my voice and proclaim that I am Yours. You have called me by name, and You have sealed my destiny in covenant love. I decree that fear is broken off my life, for You are with me in every storm, every flood, and every fire.

Lord, I dismantle every lie of the enemy that says my pain will consume me. By Your Word, I declare that the waters of affliction will not drown me, the rivers of sorrow will not carry me away, and the fires of adversity will not burn me. You, O Lord, are my shield, my Comforter, and my Deliverer.

I stand in faith and declare that cycles of destruction end with me. The enemy's plots to overwhelm my family are nullified by Your nearness. You are present in the midnight hour, present in the storm, present in the trial, and Your presence is my victory.

Father, I receive the courage to walk through every season clothed in peace. I will not faint, for You are with me. I decree over my household that no affliction shall consume us, for we are redeemed and upheld by Your mighty hand.

I rise from sorrow into joy, from wounds into wholeness, from fear into unshakable faith. For You are with me, and in Your presence there is no more pain, only peace everlasting.

In Jesus' name, Amen.

WEEK 3:
HEALING & RESTORATION

Theme: *Repairing What Was Broken.*

God does not merely acknowledge our pain—He heals it. His desire is not for us to live half-broken, barely surviving. He is the Restorer who rebuilds ruins, the Healer who binds up wounds, and the Redeemer who takes what was shattered and makes it whole again. Restoration is His promise, and healing is His gift.

The enemy's strategy is always to steal, kill, and destroy, but Jesus came to give life—abundant, restored, overflowing life. Where the enemy inflicted scars, God pours out oil. Where despair tried to settle, God plants hope. Where affliction sought to cripple, God raises strength. No wound is too deep, no loss too great, no fracture too wide for His healing hand.

This week, you will step into prayers that confront brokenness head-on. They are not just prayers of relief but of rebuilding. They call on God's power to restore health, relationships, dreams, and identities that pain tried to erase. Expect to feel the Spirit breathe new life into places you thought were finished. Healing and restoration are not a wish—they are your inheritance in Christ.

DAY 15

BEAUTY FOR ASHES

"To proclaim the year of Yahweh's favor, and the day of vengeance of our God; to comfort all who mourn; to provide for those who mourn in Zion, to give to them a garland for ashes, the oil of joy for mourning, and the garment of praise for the spirit of heaviness; that they may be called trees of righteousness, the planting of Yahweh, that he may be glorified."
— Isaiah 61:2-3 WEB

O Lord of glory and healing, I lift my heart before You with boldness today. I declare that every shroud of mourning that has covered my life and my family is now torn apart by Your mighty hand. You are the God who exchanges ashes for beauty, and I proclaim that the cycle of grief, loss, and despair is broken over my household.

Father, by Your decree, I put on the garment of praise in place of heaviness. Every generational chain of sorrow, every lingering cloud of pain, and every demonic weight of despair is consumed by Your fire. We are not children of mourning, but children of righteousness planted by the Lord Himself.

I declare that the oil of joy flows upon us now. My family shall no longer bow under affliction but stand strong as oaks of righteousness, unmovable and unbreakable. I decree that our sorrow will not return, for You have marked us as Your planting to bring You glory.

Lord, let every dark night of pain yield to the dawn of gladness. Let every tear be wiped away, and let every spirit of despair flee from our dwelling. May Your joy become our fortress and Your presence our unshakable foundation.

Today, I decree prophetically: no more pain, no more mourning, no more captivity. We arise as healed, restored, and radiant vessels of praise to the honor of Your great name.

In Jesus' name, Amen.

DAY 16

RESTORED TO HEALTH

"For I will restore health to you, and I will heal you of your wounds," says Yahweh; "because they have called you an outcast, saying, 'It is Zion, whom no man seeks after.'"
— Jeremiah 30:17 WEB

Great Healer and Restorer, I lift my voice with power and faith. You, O Lord, are the One who takes what is broken and makes it whole again. Today I declare over my life and my family that every wound—emotional, physical, or spiritual—is healed by the hand of the Lord.

Every label of rejection, every word that has branded us as forsaken or forgotten, I command to be reversed now in Jesus' name. No longer shall we be called outcasts, for the Lord Himself has sought us, healed us, and embraced us. Every scar that once bore witness of pain is transformed into a testimony of Your unfailing mercy.

Father, restore health to our bodies, peace to our minds, and wholeness to our spirits. Let every tormenting sickness, every affliction, every generational curse of infirmity be consumed by Your healing fire. I declare divine immunity against cycles of disease and decree that vitality and strength flow through every member of my household.

O God of covenant, uproot despair and plant restoration. Let wounds inflicted by betrayal, trauma, and loss be fully healed. Let every broken place be rebuilt stronger than before, a monument to Your redeeming love.

Today, I release prophetic declaration: pain has no more dominion, wounds are healed, and restoration has come. We rise in wholeness and wellness, declaring, "The Lord has healed us, and we are made whole."

In Jesus' name, Amen.

DAY 17

THE LORD WHO HEALS YOU

He said, "If you will diligently listen to Yahweh your God's voice, and will do that which is right in his eyes, and will pay attention to his commandments, and keep all his statutes, I will put none of the diseases on you, which I have put on the Egyptians; for I am Yahweh who heals you."
— Exodus 15:26 WEB

Jehovah Rapha, my Healer, I proclaim today that You are the God who heals and delivers. With lifted hands and unwavering faith, I decree that every disease, every affliction, and every generational plague assigned against me and my family is destroyed by Your power. You are the covenant-keeping God who has promised wholeness to those who walk with You.

Lord, I renounce the curses of sickness that have tried to track my lineage. Every spirit of infirmity that has sought to bind us, I command it to depart in the mighty name of Jesus. No more cycles of affliction, no more repeated diagnoses, no more inherited pain.

Father, I align my heart with Your Word. As I give heed to Your voice and walk in Your ways, let the floodgates of healing be released over every area of my life. Heal my bloodline, cleanse my DNA, and renew every organ, bone, and cell with the breath of Your Spirit.

I proclaim that in my household, there shall be no premature death, no chronic suffering, no affliction that lingers. The blood of Jesus speaks better things, and it speaks healing over every child, every parent, every generation connected to me.

Today, I stand as a prophetic voice declaring: no more pain, no more disease, no more defeat. We are sealed under the covenant of health and life because You are Yahweh who heals us.

In Jesus' name, Amen.

DAY 18

CROWNED WITH LOVING KINDNESS

"Praise Yahweh, my soul, and don't forget all his benefits; who forgives all your sins; who heals all your diseases; who redeems your life from destruction; who crowns you with loving kindness and tender mercies."
— Psalm 103:2-4 WEB

Mighty Redeemer, I bless Your holy name with all that is within me. You are the One who forgives, heals, redeems, and crowns. I declare that my life and the lives of my family are covered by Your benefits, and no demonic power can revoke what You have decreed.

Father, I thank You that every sin and transgression is blotted out by the blood of Jesus. Because of Your mercy, the accuser has no legal right to torment us with guilt or shame. I proclaim full deliverance from condemnation, and I decree that healing flows freely where sin once opened doors to affliction.

Lord, redeem our lives from every trap of destruction. Break every assignment of death, every plot of the enemy to cut short destinies, and every shadow of disaster hanging over my household. Let the fire of Your redemption consume every snare.

I decree that my family is crowned with loving-kindness. We shall not wear crowns of sorrow, but crowns of mercy and peace. We walk under the covering of Your compassion, immune from the arrows of despair and destruction.

I release prophetic victory: our sins are forgiven, our diseases are healed, our lives are redeemed, and our heads are crowned with mercy. From this day forward, the song of deliverance shall never leave our lips.

In Jesus' name, Amen.

DAY 19

YEARS RESTORED

"I will restore to you the years that the swarming locust has eaten, the great locust, the grasshopper, and the caterpillar, my great army, which I sent among you."
— Joel 2:25 WEB

Ancient of Days, I lift a decree of restoration over my life. You are the God who redeems lost years and wasted seasons. Every time stolen by sorrow, every opportunity devoured by pain, every blessing eaten by the enemy is now restored in full measure.

Father, I declare that my family shall no longer live in the shadow of loss. Where the enemy sought to destroy our harvest, You now multiply abundance. Where he devoured health, You restore vitality. Where he drained joy, You pour out gladness in overflowing supply.

I release prophetic reversal over every devouring spirit. No longer shall locusts consume our fruit, no longer shall time slip into emptiness, and no longer shall our generations be bound by cycles of barrenness. Every wasted year is gathered back by the hand of the Restorer.

Lord, restore not only the years but the glory of those years. Let honor, wealth, peace, and strength rise again. Let laughter echo where silence of despair once reigned. Let the inheritance of my family shine brighter than it ever did before.

I proclaim it boldly: no more pain, no more loss, no more wasted seasons. Our years are restored, our harvests multiplied, and our legacy secured in Your covenant faithfulness.

In Jesus' name, Amen.

DAY 20

PRAYER OF FAITH

"Is any among you sick? Let him call for the elders of the assembly, and let them pray over him, anointing him with oil in the name of the Lord, and the prayer of faith will heal him who is sick, and the Lord will raise him up. If he has committed sins, he will be forgiven."
— James 5:14-15 WEB

Lord of mercy and power, I lift a prophetic decree of faith over my life and my family. I proclaim that sickness shall not prevail, for the prayer of faith releases divine healing. Today, I stand as one anointed with Your Spirit, declaring restoration for every broken body and weary soul.

Father, I call forth heavenly oil upon my household. Let the anointing destroy every yoke of affliction. Let fevers break, tumors dissolve, and chronic ailments vanish under the authority of Jesus' name. Let every sickbed turn into a testimony of resurrection life.

I decree that the Lord Himself raises us up. Every low place of weakness, every pit of despair, every season of incapacity is overturned by Your resurrection power. We will not be bowed down by disease, but lifted high into wholeness and vitality.

Lord, where sin has opened doors to infirmity, I decree forgiveness by the blood of Jesus. Every accusation is silenced, every curse revoked, and every guilt shattered. Your mercy triumphs over judgment, and Your healing flows like living water.

Today, I release a prophetic verdict: no more pain, no more sickness, no more defeat. The prayer of faith has prevailed, the oil of the Spirit has healed, and the Lord has raised us up.

In Jesus' name, Amen.

DAY 21

BY HIS STRIPES

"Who his own self bore our sins in his body on the tree,
that we, having died to sins, might live to righteousness.
You were healed by his wounds."
— 1 Peter 2:24 WEB

Lion of Judah, I roar forth this decree of victory: by the wounds of Christ, I am healed! Today, I stand in covenant with the blood-soaked cross and declare that my life and family are fully covered.

Lord Jesus, You bore the crushing weight of sin and pain so that we would not remain bound. I proclaim that every sickness, every disease, every curse of infirmity was nailed to the cross with You. No cycle of suffering can rise against the stripes that purchased our healing.

I command pain to leave, brokenness to flee, and weakness to dissolve. In my family, bodies are restored, minds renewed, and spirits set free. Every satanic assault of sickness finds no place, for Your wounds have already secured our wholeness.

Father, I decree that we live to righteousness. No longer will sin's dominion open doors to torment. We stand clothed in the righteousness of Christ, immune to the enemy's claims.

Prophetically, I declare: the blood speaks better things than pain, the cross silences every sickness, and the stripes of Jesus establish our covenant of healing. No more pain, no more captivity—only life, peace, and wellness flow through us forevermore. In Jesus' name, Amen.

DAY 22

THE GOD WHO HEARS

"For the people will live in Zion at Jerusalem. You will weep no more. He will surely be gracious to you at the voice of your cry. When he hears you, he will answer you."
— Isaiah 30:19 WEB

O God who hears, I cry out today with holy boldness. I decree that the days of weeping in my life and family are ended. Your Word declares that You hear the voice of my cry, and I proclaim with certainty that divine answers are being released now.

Father, let every tear sown in pain be turned into a harvest of joy. Every night of mourning is silenced, every season of anguish closed, and every sound of sorrow broken forever. You are gracious to me, and I declare that my cry has reached Your throne.

I decree that the heavens are open over my household. Angelic responses are dispatched, deliverance is executed, and healing manifests speedily. No more silence, no more delay, no more unanswered cries—Your mercy has prevailed.

Lord, let Zion be our dwelling place, a city of peace and restoration. I declare that my family shall not dwell in exile, affliction, or despair, but in the place of Your covenant promises. The atmosphere of our home is filled with answered prayer and testimonies of joy.

Prophetically, I release this decree: no more pain, no more tears, no more unanswered cries. The God who hears has answered, and we shall live in wholeness and peace forevermore. In Jesus' name, Amen.

WEEK 4:
WHOLENESS & HOPE

Theme: *Joy, Renewal, and Forward Freedom.*

The journey does not end with healing—it leads into wholeness. Wholeness is more than the absence of pain; it is the fullness of peace. It is living in joy that is not fragile, walking in hope that does not fade, and standing in freedom that cannot be stolen. God's ultimate promise is not just to mend our wounds but to establish us in lasting renewal.

Hope is the anchor of this final section. It points us forward, beyond what was lost, into what God has prepared. Revelation declares that a day is coming with no more tears, no more death, no more sorrow. That eternal promise begins even now, as His presence reshapes our lives. He does not just patch up brokenness—He redefines our future.

This week's prayers are filled with expectation. They declare joy over despair, light over darkness, and new beginnings over endings. They speak wholeness over your body, mind, spirit, and household. As you press into them, see yourself stepping into a season where pain no longer dictates your story. Wholeness and hope are your reality, and forward freedom is your portion in Christ.

DAY 23

EVERLASTING LIGHT OF JOY

"The sun will be no more your light by day, nor will the brightness of the moon give light to you, but Yahweh will be your everlasting light, and your God will be your glory. Your sun will not go down any more, nor will your moon withdraw itself; for Yahweh will be your everlasting light, and the days of your mourning will end."
— Isaiah 60:19-20 WEB

Almighty Father, the God of endless light and unfading glory, I lift my voice to declare that the reign of darkness has ended in my life and my household. I proclaim with authority that every shadow of grief, every cycle of sorrow, and every night of torment is broken by the brilliance of Your everlasting presence. Your light now governs my path, and Your glory overshadows every remnant of despair.

Lord of Hosts, drive out every spiritual enemy that feeds on mourning and pain. I decree that no curse of the enemy shall dim the radiance You have ignited within me. Let the consuming fire of Your Spirit uproot sorrow, depression, and hopelessness. By Your Word, mourning has expired, and joy has taken its place.

My God, You are my glory, my covering, and my crown. I will no longer bow to the spirits of affliction that attempt to chain my family to yesterday's pain. Every generational sorrow is overturned. I decree that my household stands clothed in divine radiance, immune to the cycles of night.

Today I embrace the dawn of healing, restoration, and forward freedom. The sun of righteousness has risen with healing in His wings over my life. My destiny will not wither, my spirit will not grow faint, and my future will not fade, for You are my everlasting light.

Father, let Your light shine upon me so brilliantly that every hidden enemy is exposed and destroyed. Let Your eternal radiance be the atmosphere of my life, chasing away sorrow forever. I step boldly into the realm of unending joy and peace.

In Jesus' name, Amen.

DAY 24

JOY INSTEAD OF WEEPING

"I will rejoice in Jerusalem, and take delight in my people; and the voice of weeping and of crying will be heard in her no more."
— Isaiah 65:19 WEB

O God of comfort and delight, I rise in faith to declare that the voice of weeping has been silenced in my life. The sound of grief will no longer echo through my home, for You have decreed joy as my portion. I align myself with Your promise that tears shall not define me, and pain shall not reign in my household.

Mighty Deliverer, silence every power that thrives on sorrow. I come against every demonic assignment designed to perpetuate grief in my family. By the authority of Your Word, I uproot despair, rejection, and mourning from our midst. Let the rivers of gladness wash away the residue of pain and establish a fountain of rejoicing in our hearts.

Lord, You delight in me, and because You delight in me, enemies of peace cannot prevail. Every spiritual thief that steals laughter from my children and drains hope from my marriage is cast down. You are planting songs of triumph where tears once fell.

I decree that our dwelling place will no longer echo with sorrow but resound with the praises of the redeemed. Father, let divine celebration replace every funeral dirge of the past. Let breakthroughs roar louder than any lament.

Your delight in me becomes my shield. I live in the joy of Your covenant, walking in peace unshaken by trials. My household will flourish in laughter, dancing in the light of Your presence forevermore.

In Jesus' name, Amen.

DAY 25

OVERFLOW OF GLADNESS

"They will come and sing in the height of Zion, and will flow to the goodness of Yahweh, to the grain, to the new wine, and to the oil, and to the young of the flock and of the herd. Their soul will be as a watered garden. They will not sorrow any more at all. Then the virgin will rejoice in the dance, and the young men and the old together; for I will turn their mourning into joy, and will comfort them, and make them rejoice from their sorrow. I will satiate the soul of the priests with fatness, and my people will be satisfied with my goodness, says Yahweh."
— Jeremiah 31:12-14 WEB

Great Shepherd of Israel, I declare that my soul is a watered garden, refreshed by the streams of Your presence. I will no longer live in the barrenness of sorrow, for You have appointed joy and overflowing gladness as my inheritance.

Lord, I decree that my household will be filled with songs of celebration. The chains of grief are shattered, and the mourning cloths are burned in Your holy fire. Every enemy that once rejoiced at our sorrow is defeated, for You have turned our lament into dancing.

Mighty Redeemer, let the oil of gladness saturate my spirit and destroy the heaviness of despair. Let the wine of joy overflow in my life and in the generations to come. I proclaim that my family and I will never be starved of Your goodness. Where the enemy once planted lack, You now pour out abundance.

Father, fill my home with holy laughter. Let every heart be strengthened, young and old alike, as we rejoice in You. We step into the season of rejoicing, unshaken by trials, undisturbed by losses.

Lord of comfort, You are my satisfaction. You fill me with wholeness, and You saturate my life with peace. No more pain, no more sorrow—only the goodness of Yahweh shall flow continually in my dwelling.

In Jesus' name, Amen.

DAY 26

REST FOR THE WEARY

"Come to me, all you who labor and are heavily burdened, and I will give you rest. Take my yoke upon you, and learn from me, for I am gentle and humble in heart; and you will find rest for your souls. For my yoke is easy, and my burden is light."
— Matthew 11:28-30 WEB

Lord Jesus, Gentle Shepherd of my soul, I run into Your embrace with a heart weary from battles and burdens. Today I declare that I will not carry the weight of sorrow or the yoke of pain any longer. You have offered me Your rest, and I receive it by faith.

I break every chain of heavy labor that the enemy has tried to bind around my family. Every generational curse of striving, exhaustion, and endless cycles of affliction is destroyed by the power of Your Word. I cast off the burdens of grief and oppression and step into the rest that only You can give.

Lord, You are gentle and humble in heart, and You teach me the way of peace. Deliver me from the harsh taskmasters of fear, anxiety, and despair. Let every tormentor be driven out by the authority of Your presence. Replace my turmoil with divine serenity.

Father, I embrace Your easy yoke—the yoke of love, grace, and covenant rest. I decree that my family shall no longer be crushed under burdens too heavy to bear. We enter into a season of peace, where pain is broken and wholeness is established.

I will walk with confidence, knowing You carry the weight of my destiny. In You, there is no more pain, only peace that surpasses understanding. Your rest is my inheritance.

In Jesus' name, Amen.

DAY 27

NO MORE TEARS FOREVER

"He will wipe away from them every tear from their eyes.
Death will be no more; neither will there be mourning,
nor crying, nor pain, any more. The first things have
passed away."
— Revelation 21:4 WEB

Lord of Eternity, I lift my voice in triumph, declaring that sorrow
has no lasting power over me. Your Word decrees the end of pain,
and I align my life with this eternal promise. You are wiping away
every tear, and the residue of grief is erased forever.

O God of comfort, destroy the works of every spirit that thrives on
death and mourning. Let the forces that bring torment and anguish
be cast into the abyss. In my life and in my family, we will not be
bound by cycles of loss. The former things are passed away, and all
things are made new in You.

Lord Jesus, You conquered death, You triumphed over pain, and
You silenced the grave. I decree that Your victory becomes the
atmosphere of my life. Sorrow cannot dwell here. Fear cannot reign
here. The curse of pain has expired in the light of Your glory.

Father, make my home a sanctuary of joy. Let laughter echo where
tears once fell. Let new beginnings flourish where endings once
brought despair. I decree that every enemy of peace is crushed
under the weight of Christ's triumph.

God of new creation, I receive the fullness of life everlasting. My family and I shall live in the wholeness of Your promise, free from pain, fear, and sorrow. No more tears, no more death, no more mourning—only eternal joy in Your presence.

In Jesus' name, Amen.

DAY 28

ALL THINGS WORK TOGETHER

"We know that all things work together for good for those who love God, to those who are called according to his purpose."
— Romans 8:28 WEB

Sovereign Lord, I stand in faith to decree that every trial, every wound, and every tear is now working for my good. You are weaving my pain into purpose, and You are turning sorrow into strength. My life and my family's destiny are secured in Your eternal plan.

Father, I silence the lies of the enemy that declare defeat over my journey. I uproot the spirit of despair that whispers hopelessness. Every scheme of darkness is overturned by Your divine orchestration. What the enemy meant for harm, You are transforming into testimony.

Lord, I love You with all my heart, and I walk in the calling You have ordained. Because I am called, affliction cannot hold me captive. Because I am Yours, every disappointment must bow to Your greater purpose. My setbacks are becoming stepping stones, my scars are becoming songs of victory.

I decree that my family will live in the reality of Your goodness. Even the painful chapters of our story will be redeemed for glory. Father, raise beauty from ashes, and let the fragrance of Your grace fill every broken place.

You are the God who restores and renews. I declare that no sorrow is wasted, no wound is ignored. All things, even the hardest battles, are working together to display Your faithfulness.

In Jesus' name, Amen.

DAY 29

RESTORER OF MY SOUL

"He restores my soul. He guides me in the paths of righteousness for his name's sake."
— Psalm 23:3 WEB

Lord, my Shepherd and Healer, I declare that my soul is restored by Your mighty hand. Where pain once drained me, You are pouring out renewal. Where sorrow once weighed me down, You are lifting me up into wholeness.

Father, I come against every spiritual enemy that has targeted my soul with despair, trauma, and heaviness. I decree that no force of darkness will have dominion over my inner being. My emotions, my mind, and my spirit are sanctified and strengthened by Your presence.

Lord, You guide me into righteousness. I will not be led by confusion, nor trapped by cycles of error. Every generational path of brokenness is destroyed, and I now walk in the divine order of peace and restoration.

Mighty Redeemer, breathe new life into my heart. Restore joy where grief once ruled. Heal the wounds of the past and silence the voices of regret. I decree that my soul is no longer fractured but whole, vibrant, and free.

Because of Your name, I will not stumble. Because of Your glory, I will not fail. You restore me continually, and You lead me securely into the destiny You have prepared. In Jesus' name, Amen.

DAY 30

HE TOOK MY INFIRMITIES

"When evening came, they brought to him many possessed with demons. He cast out the spirits with a word, and healed all who were sick, that it might be fulfilled which was spoken through Isaiah the prophet, saying: 'He took our infirmities and bore our diseases.'"
— Matthew 8:16-17 WEB

Lord Jesus, Mighty Deliverer, I declare that You have already carried my pain and borne my afflictions. By the authority of Your finished work, every sickness, every sorrow, and every demonic oppression is broken off my life and my family.

I decree that infirmity has no right to dwell in our bodies. Every spirit of disease, every assignment of chronic pain, and every weapon of affliction is destroyed by Your Word. You healed them all, and I receive that same healing power today.

Lord, You cast out spirits with a word, and I decree that every unclean power tormenting my household flees at Your command. Depression, anxiety, sickness, and generational infirmities are uprooted and banished from our lineage.

Father, I embrace the divine exchange of the cross. You bore my grief so I could live in joy. You carried my pain so I could walk in peace. No enemy can reattach what You have removed, and no curse can revive what You have already nailed to the cross.

I stand in wholeness, declaring healing over my body, my mind, and my family. Pain is overthrown, and wellness is established. We live in the fullness of Your redemption.

In Jesus' name, Amen.

Epilogue

As you close this book, may you feel the weight of old burdens lifting from your heart. What once seemed permanent—pain, sorrow, and cycles of despair—has been met by the unchanging power of God. You have not only read prayers, but you have walked through a journey of encounter, invitation, and transformation. The God who knows every wound has met you in every place of brokenness, and His presence continues to linger, steadying your steps and whispering peace over your spirit.

Take this truth with you: your past does not define your future. Every sorrow that sought to claim your life has been broken, every hidden wound has been brought into the healing light of God's love, and every fear has been met with His protective hand. The God who carried you through these pages will continue to walk with you—through trials, uncertainties, and moments when pain tries to reappear. You are held, redeemed, and empowered to live fully in His wholeness.

Let the prayers you have prayed become a daily shield, a reminder that you are never alone in your struggles. Let the Scriptures you've meditated on anchor your hope, fortify your faith, and renew your strength. As you step forward, carry the joy of restoration, the courage of freedom, and the authority of Christ over every lingering shadow in your life and your family.

Your story of healing does not end here. It is only beginning. May your days be marked by peace that passes understanding, by strength that rises from weakness, and by the abiding presence of the God who turns every pain into a testimony of glory.

In Jesus' name, Amen.

ENCOURAGE OTHERS WITH YOUR STORY

If this prayer guide has strengthened your faith, deepened your intercession, or helped you stand in the gap, would you consider leaving a short review on Amazon? Your feedback not only encourages others but also helps more believers discover this resource and join in the prayer movement. Every review—just a few sentences—makes a difference. Thank you for being part of this movement.

MORE FROM PRAYERSCRIPTS

COMMAND YOUR DESTINY SERIES

Command Your Morning:

30 Days of Prayers and Declarations to Seize Your Day and Shape Your Destiny

There is a battle over every morning—and every believer must choose to either drift into the day or command it.

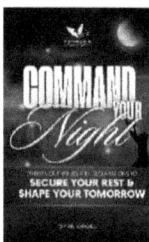

Command Your Night:

30 Days of Prayers and Declarations to Secure Your Rest and Shape Your Tomorrow

Every night is a spiritual battlefield—what you do before you sleep can determine the course of your tomorrow.

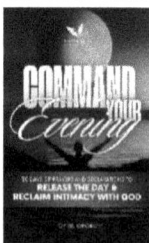

Command Your Evening:

30 Days of Prayers and Declarations to Release the Day and Reclaim Intimacy with God

There is a battle over every transition—and evening is one of the most spiritually neglected.

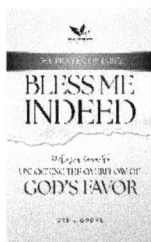

Bless Me Indeed:

Unlocking the Overflow of God's Favor

What if you could activate God's favor in your life today and walk in blessings that surpass your wildest expectations?

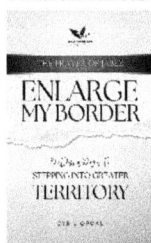

Enlarge My Border:

Stepping Into Greater Territory

Do you feel like you're living beneath your full potential? Do limitations, setbacks, and invisible barriers keep you from stepping into all God has promised? It's time to lift your cry for enlargement.

May Your Hand Be With Me:

Living Under Divine Power and Presence

What happens when the mighty hand of God rests upon your life? Doors open that no man can shut. Strength rises where weakness once prevailed. Guidance comes in the midst of confusion, and protection surrounds you in every battle.

Keep Me From Evil:

Standing Untouchable in Spiritual Warfare

What if the enemy's plans could never touch you or your family? Imagine walking through life completely protected, untouchable, and victorious—no matter what schemes are formed against you.

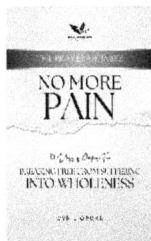

No More Pain:

Breaking Free from Suffering into Wholeness

Have you been carrying the weight of sorrow, disappointment, or hidden wounds for far too long? Do cycles of pain seem to repeat in your life, your marriage, or your family?

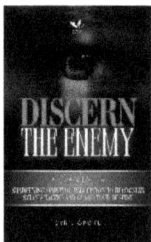

Discern the Enemy:

Sharpening Spiritual Perception to Recognize Satan's Tactics and Guard Your Destiny

The greatest danger is not the enemy you can see—it is the one you cannot. Can you recognize the enemy before he strikes?

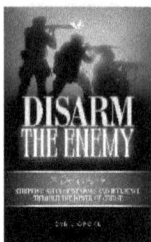

Disarm the Enemy:

Stripping Satan of Weapons and Influence Through the Power of Christ

Are you tired of feeling like the enemy has the upper hand in your life? It's time to take back your ground, silence the lies of darkness, and walk in the unstoppable authority of Christ.

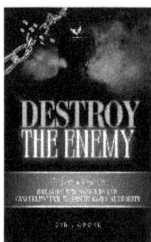

Destroy the Enemy:

Breaking Strongholds and Cancelling Evil Works by God's Authority

Are you tired of living under the weight of unseen battles? It's time to rise up and destroy the enemy's works in your life.

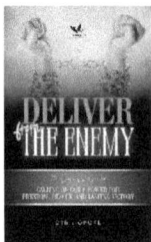

Deliver from the Enemy:

Calling on God's Power for Freedom, Rescue, and Lasting Victory

Break free from spiritual attacks and experience God's mighty deliverance in every battle.

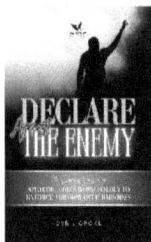

Declare Against the Enemy:

Speaking God's Word Boldly to Enforce Triumph Over Darkness

What if you could silence the enemy's schemes, protect your family, and walk boldly into every God-ordained assignment with unshakable authority?

Scriptures & Prayers for Deliverance from Trouble:

40 Days of Prayer for When Life Feels Overwhelming

Are you walking through a season where life feels heavy and your prayers feel weak?

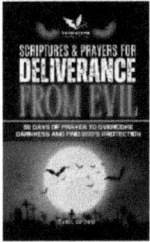

Scriptures & Prayers for Deliverance from Evil:

50 Days of Prayer to Overcome Darkness and Find God's Protection

When darkness presses in, how do you pray?

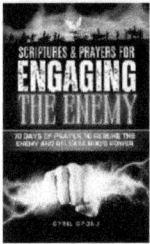

Scriptures & Prayers for Engaging the Enemy:

70 Days of Prayer to Rebuke the Enemy and Release God's Power

You weren't called to run from the battle—you were anointed to win it.

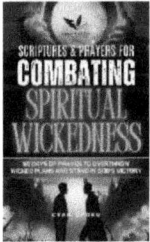

Scriptures & Prayers for Combating Spiritual Wickedness:

50 Days of Prayer to Overthrow Wicked Plans and Stand in God's Victory

Are you facing opposition that feels deeper than the natural? You're not imagining it—and you're not powerless.

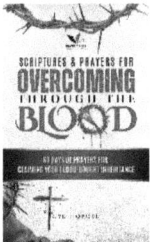

Scriptures & Prayers for Overcoming Through the Blood:

60 Days of Prayers for Claiming Your Blood-Bought Inheritance

You were never meant to fight sin, fear, or Satan in your own strength.

Standing in the Gap for Covenant Awakening:

30 Days of Prayer for National Repentance, Righteous Leadership & God's Sovereign Rule

What if your prayers could help turn the tide of a nation?

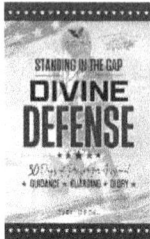

Standing in the Gap for Divine Defense:

30 Days of Prayer for National Guidance, Guarding & Glory

When the foundations of a nation feel as if they're shaking, prayer is the strongest fortress you can build.

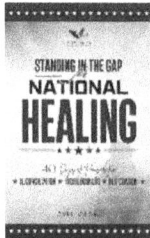

Standing in the Gap for National Healing:

40 Days of Prayer for Reconciliation, Righteousness, and Restoration

What if your prayers could help heal a nation? What if God is waiting for someone—like you—to stand in the gap?

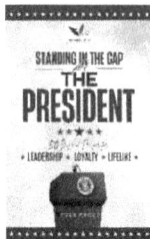

Standing in the Gap for The President:

50 Days of Prayer for Leadership, Loyalty, and Lifeline

When a nation's leader is under spiritual siege, will you answer the call to stand in the gap?

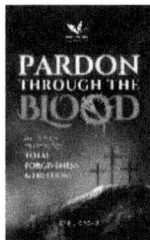

Pardon Through the Blood:

60 Days of Prayers for Total Forgiveness and Freedom

Guilt is a prison. The blood of Jesus holds the key.

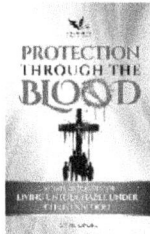

Protection Through the Blood:

60 Days of Prayers for Living Untouchable Under Christ's Blood

You are not helpless. You are not exposed. You are covered—completely—by the blood of Jesus.

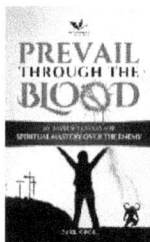

Prevail Through the Blood:

60 Days of Prayers for Spiritual Mastery Over the Enemy

What if every scheme of the enemy against your life could be dismantled—by one unstoppable weapon?

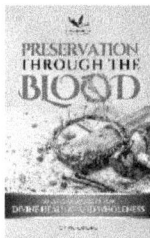

Preservation Through the Blood:

60 Days of Prayers for Divine Healing and Wholeness

Unlock Lasting Healing and Wholeness Through the Blood of Jesus

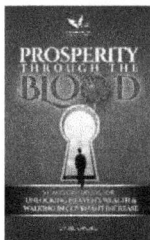

Prosperity Through the Blood:

60 Days of Prayers for Unlocking Heaven's Wealth and Walking in Covenant Increase

You were redeemed for more than survival—you were redeemed to prosper.

Peace Through the Blood:

60 Days of Prayers for Resting in the Covenant of Unshakable Peace

Are you ready to silence every storm of the mind, heart, and home—once and for all?

www.ingramcontent.com/pod-product-compliance
Lightning Source LLC
Chambersburg PA
CBHW062024040426
42447CB00010B/2128